Rewriting Financial Rules!

Simple keys to rewriting financial rules using
credit repairing, building,
and consumer reporting strategies.

Darius Norman, MSW

Rewriting Financial Rules! © 2016
Darius Norman, MSW
82 Blankenship Place
Rome, Georgia 30165

References:
Investopedia
The National Foundation for Credit Counseling
Scott Hilton
My Fico
Wikipedia
Howard Dayton, Crown Financial

ISBN: 978-0-692-78671-0

Acknowledgments

First, I acknowledge God, who is the Captain of my life and who appointed this great task to me. This book is dedicated to my family and closest friends who encouraged me as I personally traveled this path of discovery, perseverance, faith, hope, and determination to conquer my own financial challenges. In lending me their support, I am able to be open with you on the next few pages to offer you some level of hope.

Thank you!

In Gratitude

The following individuals I offer a special 'thanks' for their support of this work. Their encouragement and generosity were very instrumental in its completion.

"Let there be a never- ending flow of peace, health and wealth in all of your lives!"

John B. Norman, Jr	George Mc Donald
Raven Norman	Deloris G. Norman
Troy Norman	Vince Vickers
Michelle Jenkins	Electra E.J. Adams
John T. Norman	

Table of Contents

Introduction & Overview

As a young man, I had goals for my life that were very important for me to achieve; with these goals, I also had extreme credit issues. Due to these issues and financial woes, my goals seemed unattainable. I decided to take action instead of becoming a victim of my circumstances.

I was raised in an upper middle class family where my parents were well disciplined in their finances. The fact that I had been raised in such an atmosphere was no affirmation that I had mastered these principles and attributes for myself.

During my days in college I was introduced to another world of finances which set me on a road of disaster.

As a freshman, the environment and population defined what most young people would call success. Being surrounded by such extravagance for me was great peer-pressure and I developed poor financial habits. I struggled to maintain an image that I could not afford even after I graduated.

College surrounded me with many students who came from families ranging from upper middle-class to the extremely wealthy. Many were the elite, rich African-American children of movie stars, doctors, and professional football and basketball players.

I continued to feel pressure to perform not realizing that I was in a direct pathway to crashing with my finances. A healthy, strong self-image is imperative to survive an atmosphere of this type.

Entering graduate school, I met a young lady and fell in love as the story goes. Unfortunately, the love of my life didn't fall in love with me. My spending escalated while trying to pacify my wounded heart. This spending, including my student loans landed me in serious debt that I simply could not afford.

Even though I had a satisfying job with benefits and a great salary, I could not maintain my daily expenses. It wasn't long before I received a new job assignment that I began to analyze my financial situation and made a quality decision to begin repairing my credit.

Struggling with my credit and financial problems was not easy at all! However, with my faith strongly rooted in God, I began leaning on Him for guidance. I gained insight and learned concepts that were instrumental in changing my financial and credit situation. I knew God had given His people a plan to become financially successful. By placing Him at the head of the chart, I began my strategy.

My purpose and hope for this book is to empower people with strategies to change negative credit and financial situations; and to show others that they can come out of their situation and see change by utilizing these educational tools and making an unwavering personal commitment.

We are living in uncertain times when transitions are swift and the effects can be devastating. It is a challenge to execute strategies to ensure that when it comes to your finances, you are making smart decisions. The following steps will assist you in building a strong foundation.

(1) You need a clear view on what and whom you owe. Take a moment and list all debts, include on this list student loans, all credit cards balances, a mortgage, if you have one, the car, other loans or past due bills,

(2) During this season of clean-up, eliminate all unnecessary spending, limit dinners out. Spend only on need/necessity.

Question: So, what should I do with the extra money saved? Answer: Work toward paying off your smallest balance first. When it is paid off, begin using this strategy to subdue all debts. Using this process will offer great progress, until all debts have been conquered. Do not accumulate new credit card debt! Otherwise, you are defeated.

After paying off your credit cards begin paying off your consumer debts such as your car notes and then your largest which would probably be your home. Pay extra on your principal payments. Make every extra penny count toward your goal. Periodically review your debt-free progress. Keep a journal. *Don't forget to consider monthly income and expenses. Remember, your budget and goal tells your money where to go! *Do not leave space to wonder where it went! As you continue your path to becoming debt free, challenges might occur and adjustments might be needed. Make every effort to manage your money wisely.

Darius Norman, MSW

What is a Credit Report?

A credit report is a detailed report of an individual's credit history. The credit bureaus collect information and create credit reports based on that information, and lenders use the reports along with other details to generate a credit score.

A credit score is a number representing the credit worthiness of the person. A credit score is primarily based on a credit report information provided from the credit bureaus.

What makes up a Credit Score?

Data from your credit report goes into five major categories that make up a credit/fico score.

1. Payment History: Comprise of 35 percent of the total credit score

2. Credit Utilization: Comprise of 30 percent of the total credit score. The first two factors make up nearly two-thirds of your score. So, if you pay your bills on time and don't carry big balances, you're two thirds of the way towards a good credit score.

3. Length of Credit History: Comprise of 15 percent of the total credit score and is based on the length of time each account has been open and the length of time since the account's most recent action.

4. New Credit: Comprise of 10 percent of the total credit score.

5. Credit Mix: Comprise of 10 percent of the total credit score.

What is Credit Repair?

Credit repair is the process of identifying errors and disputing the information.

Investopedia indicated as many as 79% of consumers have some kind of error or inaccuracies on their credit report. In my research, I learned that people can be highly impacted, but are less involved with reviewing and monitoring their credit reports and scores.

According to research credit repair has become a necessary process for keeping a consumer's financial life healthy. Negative reporting and inaccuracies found on a consumer's credit report may prohibit or delay them from attaining their dreams and goals. Buying a home, starting a family, building a business, or even purchasing a car might prove to be difficult or impossible.

Furthermore, many Americans take a hands-off approach to their credit scores. The National Foundation for Credit Counseling found that, sixty percent of adults had not reviewed their credit scores within the past twelve months; and sixty-five percent had not looked at their credit report within the previous year. Only twenty-nine percent had reviewed both.

What Is A Credit Bureau?

According to Investopedia, the credit bureau is an agency that researches and collects individual credit information and sells it for a fee to creditors so they can make decisions on granting loans. A credit bureau works for lending institutions to help them make loan decisions in individual cases. Typical clients for credit bureaus are banks, mortgage lenders, credit card companies, and other finance companies. Credit bureaus are not responsible for deciding whether or not a consumer should have credit extended to them; they only collect information about that individual's credit score and give that information to the lending institutions.

Reports from credit bureaus will also determine the interest rate for debtors on their loans; an individual with a higher score will likely have a better interest rate on their loan. Bureaus acquire their information from data furnishers which can be creditors, debtors, debt collection agencies or offices with public records, and court records are all available to the public. This information is generally assembled into a numerical formula that offers an assessment of the credit history of the individual in question for the use of the credit bureau clients.

Sometimes individual reports might contain negative credit score information. This can result in higher interest rates, difficulty getting loans, and possibly securing employment. The three main credit bureaus in the United States are Equifax, Transunion, and Experian.

Consumers can also be members of credit bureaus and receive the same service information about their own credit history and dispute negative reporting or inaccuracies that are identified from all three CRA'S. Consumers are entitled to receive a free credit report once a year by going to Annual Credit Report.com. This step is extremely important because consumers, need to know what is being reported to all three bureaus because all lenders do not utilize or report to all three CRA'S. Once the consumer has identified any inaccuracies on the credit reports, they have the right to dispute the item(s), online via annualcreditreport.com or mail the disputed item(s) to the CRA. A sample credit dispute letter is available at: creditsecrets.org.

The CRA'S are held accountable by the (FCRA) and FDCPA Section 807 (8) laws to ensure that they respond to a consumer's dispute and all information on a consumer's credit report is fair and accurate.

Experian
P.O. Box 4000 Allen, TX 75013
714-830-7000

Equifax Credit Information Services, Inc
P.O. Box 740256 Atlanta, Ga. 30374
800-846-5279

Transunion, LLC
P.O. Box 2000 Chester, Pa. 19022
800-916-8800

Credit Repairing Strategies

There are 2 primary forms of credit repairing:

1. Hire a credit repair agency

2. Do- it- yourself

When I was working on repairing my credit, I chose to use a credit repair service. Due to my career and daily responsibilities, it was more beneficial for me to use such a service. As a do-it-yourself option, Scott Hilton, author of the renowned book "Credit Secrets," has carefully designed self-credit repair techniques that have proven to be effective for helping people improve their scores. According to StreetInsider.com, Hilton has helped over 12,000 people with his credit training including his girlfriend's credit score of 588 to over 700 in just a few weeks. To learn more about his credit repair system, or to purchase Scott Hilton's Credit Secret, click http;//creditsecrets.org/

Credit Repair Companies

Lexington Law | 888-585-5590

- One of the oldest & most experienced credit repair services
- They work 24/7 help improve your score and get you qualified for a better loan
- They will provide credit summary reports
- High credit repair success rate

- Uniquely aligned to challenged issues with All Three Bureaus
- More than 500,00 clients served
- www.lexingtonlaw.com

CreditRepair.com | 844-259-3419

- They contact credit bureaus & creditors to challenge negative report items
- Past members got points in 4 months (On average)
- Online account & mobile app to track progress 24/7
- Very personalized service
- Improvement in score could easily justify the cost
- BBB Rating - B
- www.creditrepair.com

Sky Blue | 888-374-1062

- Great value for responsive, professional & confidential customer service
- Fast results & they work hard. They'll challenge up to 15 disputes in 35 days
- Get started in only 2 minutes with easy online process
- Risk free, 90-day money back guarantee
- https://skybluecredit.com

Credit Saints | 877-242-1554

- 90-day money back guarantee
- Personalized credit consultations
- Cancel anytime
- Personal advisor

- Very aggressive programs

The Credit People | 855-432-3040

- 24 hours' account access
- $19 low entry fee
- Free 3 credit reports and credit scores
- Cancel anytime

Park View Credit | 844-604-4316

- Schedule consultations for free
- No win No Fee Guarantee6 years of experience
- Provides credit building guidance
- Gives help for unlimited disputes
- Live chat support available
- www.parkviewcredit.com

Credit Network Assistance | 800-811-3078

- Up to 45 disputes per cycle
- Toll-free live phone support
- Unlimited disputes
- No long-term contracts
- Performance guarantee
- www.creditagenda.com

CreditFirm.net | 800-750-1416

- Professional credit repair services
- No hidden fees

- Month to month contract, cancel anytime
- Free consultation and credit evaluation
- Unlimited disputes, challenges
- http://www.creditfirm.net

National Credit Adviser | 844-215-5283

- Free consultation
- Personalized strategy provided for credit repair
- Mobile App
- See results as fast as 90 days
- www.nationalcreditadvisors.com

The Credit Pros | 55-403-7363

- Unlimited disputes
- Money back guarantee
- Pay per deletion
- ID theft restoration and insurance
- One on one consultation with FICO certified professional

Credit Building Strategies

In the following topics, I will be providing you with three powerful credit building strategies I learned and utilized as I was repairing my own credit. As I discussed earlier, credit repair can be very effective in raising your overall credit score. However, *credit building strategies* are equally important in raising your credit scores. In the system I developed while restoring my own credit, I made a wonderful discovery; credit repair and credit building strategies are a team, and both should be implemented if you wish to see a dramatic increase in your credit scores.

Secure Credit Cards

Secure credit cards are the easiest and fastest way to begin building or reestablishing credit history and credit worthiness. If you have good, bad, or no credit, you may benefit by utilizing a secure credit card. Most secure credit cards have easy terms and no credit check is involved. All you need is to have the minimal deposit. Usually, this is the maximum credit limit of the card, and meet the card company's verification standards. Here are two secure credit card companies. They are reliable and they have easy terms. If you keep a low balance on these two cards, you could see up to a 26 to 40-point increase in your credit score in approximately 30 days if you make timely payments.

Open Sky CC has a minimal deposit of $200. No credit history or minimum credit score is required for approval, and they report to all three credit bureaus. www.openskycc.com

First Progress has a minimal deposit of $300. No credit history or minimum credit score required for approval. They report to the three credit bureaus also. You can apply online by going to https://www.first-progress.com/.

Piggy Backing

Imagine what adding $15,000 in available credit and five years of perfect payment history would do to your credit score. Piggybacking, more commonly known as an authorized user, is when a person (usually the primary account holder) permits another person to use their credit account but maintains responsibility for all debt on the card, regardless of who makes the charges. The authorized user's position is to give the primary card holder the ability to add their children, spouse, friends or employees to their accounts in order that they may access the available credit line. The authorized user receives the benefits during this process whereby the account history for that credit card appears on each authorized user's credit report, and it looks like the credit card history has been there since the account was first opened. This benefit could give a person an immediate FICO credit score boost.

While you do not need to receive a physical card, or need the ability to use the credit line, you will receive the amazing benefit of having that particular credit account copied and posted on your credit report. This extreme increase in the limit to balance utilization and overall average age of the revolving accounts on your credit report gives you the biggest possible FICO score boost.

Rent Reporting

Many people who do not have much in the way of a credit history, may have a history of paying rent on time. If that information showed up on their credit reports, it might help their scores.

You cannot report rent yourself. But rent-reporting services can get your credit reports to reflect your rent payments fairly easy at a cost that can range from free to more than $40 a year.

Rental Kharma is one such rental reporting service. Their initial setup is $40, and the service is $9.95 per month. During enrollment, you can report payments made in the previous 24 months. It reports to TransUnion. If you want to utilize their service, you can go online to https://rentalalkharma.com/ or call 720-307-1466.

Credit Report Monitoring

Credit report monitoring or company tracking is the monitoring of one's credit history to detect any suspicious activity or changes. I want to encourage you to monitor all three of your credit reports to determine if you are making progress. There are credit monitoring services that will provide you with accurate updated credit information. Some are free of charge, while others may have fees so you can continue to monitor your credit.

Two such companies are:

Myfico.com is utilized by all lending and banking institutions. Instantly access your 3-bureau credit report and FICO© Scores- including the FICO© Scores most widely used in mortgage, auto and credit card lending, and the newly released FICO © Score 9.

Access updated credit reports and your most widely used FICO© Scores every quarter tract FICO© your Score 8 from each bureau on a historic tracking graph. Monitor your 3 credit reports or changes, and get FICO Score 8 updates with each new alert which detects threats to your personal information with intelligent identity theft monitoring. Restore your identity with expert identity theft features for a monthly fee of $29.99. www.myfico.com. 1-800-319-4433.

Score Sense

See all 3 scores and reports instantly! 24/7 access allows you to stay up-to-date on monthly charges from each bureau: TransUnion, Equifax, and Experian. Get alerted to change. Credit monitoring and alerts notify you of activity or changes on your report that may need your prompt attention for monthly a fee of $14.95. https://www.scoresense.com/ 1-800-972-7204.

Free Credit Monitoring Services

Credit Sesame https://www.creditsesame.com/

Credit Karma https://www.creditkarma.com/

Quizzle https://www.quizzle.com/

Consumer Reporting Strategies

In this section I will be providing you with strategies to use as a consumer to eradicate extreme credit challenges that will expedite a 30-day response from the three credit bureaus and the company that is reporting negative or derogatory information on your credit profile. I found it helpful utilizing the Consumer Financial Protection Bureau (CFPB).

According to Wikipedia, the Consumer Financial Protection Bureau is an independent agency of the Unites States government responsible for protecting the consumer in the financial sector. Its jurisdiction includes banks, credit unions, securities, firms, payday lenders, mortgage-servicing operations, fore-closure relief services, debt collectors and other financial companies operating in the United States.

The CFPB's creation was authorized by Dodd-Frank Wall Street Reform and Consumer Protection Act, whose passage in 2010 was a legislative response to the financial crisis of 2007-08 and the subsequent, Great Recession.

The Bureau is tasked with the responsibility to promote fairness and transparency for mortgages, credit reporting agencies, student loans, credit cards, and other consumer financial products and services. According to its web site, the CFPB's central mission is to make markets for consumer financial products and services work for Americans whether they are applying for a mortgage, choosing among credit cards, or using any number of other consumer financial products. The Consumer Financial Protection Bureau gives you the ability to make a complaint against the company or credit bureau that is reporting the negative item. The company must respond to your complaint within 15 business days. The process of filing a complaint is simple and easy. Log on to http://www.consumerfinancial.gov. and file your complaint. Your complaint must detail: Company name, contact information, as well as the details of the debt. It was after I learned to use the CFPB myself that I saw those stubborn credit items removed from my own credit profile more quickly than the thirty-day dispute letter challenges. I received timely responses from the companies reporting the negative items.

Twenty-One Day Credit Journal

It's a good practice to make a note of who you spoke with at any agency. This journal will help you track those calls and the dates in which you made the contact. This is also appreciated when you are in conversation with the agency later.

Date: _____

ACTIONS:

Goals I set today

_____

_____

_____

_____

Phone calls I made:	Contact Made	Appointments made:
_____	☐	_____ / _____ / _____
_____	☐	_____ / _____ / _____
_____	☐	_____ / _____ / _____
_____	☐	_____ / _____ / _____

Payments Made Toward My Goals:

_____

_____

GOALS ACHIEVED:

_____

_____

_____

_____

Date: _____

ACTIONS:

Goals I set today

_____

_____

_____

_____

Phone calls I made:	Contact Made	Appointments made:
_____	☐	____ / ____ / ____
_____	☐	____ / ____ / ____
_____	☐	____ / ____ / ____
_____	☐	____ / ____ / ____

Payments Made Toward My Goals:

_____

_____

GOALS ACHIEVED:

_____

_____

_____

_____

Date: _____

ACTIONS:

Goals I set today

_____

_____

_____

_____

Phone calls I made:	Contact Made	Appointments made:
_____	☐	____ / ____ / ____
_____	☐	____ / ____ / ____
_____	☐	____ / ____ / ____
_____	☐	____ / ____ / ____

Payments Made Toward My Goals:

_____

_____

GOALS ACHIEVED:

_____

_____

_____

_____

Date: _____

ACTIONS:

Goals I set today

_____

_____

_____

_____

Phone calls I made:	Contact Made	Appointments made:
_____	☐	_____ / _____ / _____
_____	☐	_____ / _____ / _____
_____	☐	_____ / _____ / _____
_____	☐	_____ / _____ / _____

Payments Made Toward My Goals:

_____

_____

GOALS ACHIEVED:

_____

_____

_____

_____

Date: _____

ACTIONS:

Goals I set today

_____

_____

_____

_____

Phone calls I made:	Contact Made	Appointments made:
_____	☐	___ / ___ / ___
_____	☐	___ / ___ / ___
_____	☐	___ / ___ / ___
_____	☐	___ / ___ / ___

Payments Made Toward My Goals:

_____

_____

GOALS ACHIEVED:

_____

_____

_____

_____

Date: _____

ACTIONS:

Goals I set today

_____

_____

_____

_____

Phone calls I made:	Contact Made	Appointments made:
_____	☐	___ / ___ / ___
_____	☐	___ / ___ / ___
_____	☐	___ / ___ / ___
_____	☐	___ / ___ / ___

Payments Made Toward My Goals:

_____

_____

GOALS ACHIEVED:

_____

_____

_____

_____

Date: _____

ACTIONS:

Goals I set today

_____

_____

_____

_____

Phone calls I made:	Contact Made	Appointments made:
_____	☐	___/___/___
_____	☐	___/___/___
_____	☐	___/___/___
_____	☐	___/___/___

Payments Made Toward My Goals:

_____

_____

GOALS ACHIEVED:

_____

_____

_____

_____

Date: _____

ACTIONS:

Goals I set today

_____

_____

_____

_____

Phone calls I made:	Contact Made	Appointments made:
_____	☐	____ / ____ / ____
_____	☐	____ / ____ / ____
_____	☐	____ / ____ / ____
_____	☐	____ / ____ / ____

Payments Made Toward My Goals:

_____

_____

GOALS ACHIEVED:

_____

_____

_____

Date: _____

ACTIONS:

Goals I set today

_____

_____

_____

_____

Phone calls I made:	Contact Made	Appointments made:
_____	☐	____ / ____ / ____
_____	☐	____ / ____ / ____
_____	☐	____ / ____ / ____
_____	☐	____ / ____ / ____

Payments Made Toward My Goals:

_____

_____

GOALS ACHIEVED:

_____

_____

_____

Date: _____

ACTIONS:

Goals I set today

_____

_____

_____

_____

Phone calls I made:	Contact Made	Appointments made:
_____	☐	___ / ___ / ___
_____	☐	___ / ___ / ___
_____	☐	___ / ___ / ___
_____	☐	___ / ___ / ___

Payments Made Toward My Goals:

_____

_____

GOALS ACHIEVED:

_____

_____

_____

_____

Date: _____

ACTIONS:

Goals I set today

_____

_____

_____

_____

Phone calls I made:	Contact Made	Appointments made:
_____	☐	____ / ____ / ____
_____	☐	____ / ____ / ____
_____	☐	____ / ____ / ____
_____	☐	____ / ____ / ____

Payments Made Toward My Goals:

_____

_____

GOALS ACHIEVED:

_____

_____

_____

_____

Date: _____

ACTIONS:

Goals I set today

_____

_____

_____

_____

Phone calls I made:	Contact Made	Appointments made:
_____	☐	___ / ___ / ___
_____	☐	___ / ___ / ___
_____	☐	___ / ___ / ___
_____	☐	___ / ___ / ___

Payments Made Toward My Goals:

_____

_____

GOALS ACHIEVED:

_____

_____

_____

_____

Date: _____

ACTIONS:

Goals I set today

_____

_____

_____

_____

Phone calls I made:	Contact Made	Appointments made:
_____	☐	___ / ___ / ___
_____	☐	___ / ___ / ___
_____	☐	___ / ___ / ___
_____	☐	___ / ___ / ___

Payments Made Toward My Goals:

_____

_____

GOALS ACHIEVED:

_____

_____

_____

_____

Date: _____

ACTIONS:

Goals I set today

_____

_____

_____

_____

Phone calls I made:	Contact Made	Appointments made:
_____	☐	_____ / _____ /
_____	☐	_____ / _____ /
_____	☐	_____ / _____ /
_____	☐	_____ / _____ /

Payments Made Toward My Goals:

_____

_____

GOALS ACHIEVED:

_____

_____

_____

_____

Date: _____

ACTIONS:

Goals I set today

_____

_____

_____

Phone calls I made:	Contact Made	Appointments made:
_____	☐	_____ / _____ / _____
_____	☐	_____ / _____ / _____
_____	☐	_____ / _____ / _____
_____	☐	_____ / _____ / _____

Payments Made Toward My Goals:

_____

_____

GOALS ACHIEVED:

_____

_____

_____

_____

Date: _____

ACTIONS:

Goals I set today

_____

_____

_____

_____

Phone calls I made:	Contact Made	Appointments made:
_____	☐	____ / ____ / ____
_____	☐	____ / ____ / ____
_____	☐	____ / ____ / ____
_____	☐	____ / ____ / ____

Payments Made Toward My Goals:

_____

_____

GOALS ACHIEVED:

_____

_____

_____

_____

Date: _____

ACTIONS:

Goals I set today

_____

_____

_____

_____

Phone calls I made:	Contact Made	Appointments made:
_____	☐	_____ / _____ / _____
_____	☐	_____ / _____ / _____
_____	☐	_____ / _____ / _____
_____	☐	_____ / _____ / _____

Payments Made Toward My Goals:

_____

_____

GOALS ACHIEVED:

_____

_____

_____

_____

Date: _____

ACTIONS:

Goals I set today

_____

_____

_____

_____

Phone calls I made:	Contact Made	Appointments made:
_____	☐	_____ / _____ / _____
_____	☐	_____ / _____ / _____
_____	☐	_____ / _____ / _____
_____	☐	_____ / _____ / _____

Payments Made Toward My Goals:

_____

_____

GOALS ACHIEVED:

_____

_____

_____

_____

Date: _____

ACTIONS:

Goals I set today

_____

_____

_____

_____

Phone calls I made:	Contact Made	Appointments made:
_____	☐	____ / ____ /
_____	☐	____ / ____ /
_____	☐	____ / ____ /
_____	☐	____ / ____ /

Payments Made Toward My Goals:

_____

_____

GOALS ACHIEVED:

_____

_____

_____

_____

Date: _____

ACTIONS:

Goals I set today

_____

_____

_____

_____

Phone calls I made:	Contact Made	Appointments made:	
_____	☐	_____ /	_____ /
_____	☐	_____ /	_____ /
_____	☐	_____ /	_____ /
_____	☐	_____ /	_____ /

Payments Made Toward My Goals:

_____

_____

GOALS ACHIEVED:

_____

_____

_____

About the Author

Darius Norman is a Native of Birmingham, Alabama currently living in Atlanta,Ga. He is a Social Worker with 10 years of experience working with Individuals, Families, and communities. He obtained his B.A. in Religion from Morris Brown College in 2003. And he went on to obtain his Graduate degree in Social Work from Clark Atlanta University in 2005. It has been his mission since becoming a Social Worker to empower others with a educational tool to assist them in taking control of their Financial and credit issues so they can have a stable Financial future.